My Christmas

Monica Hughes

Raintree

Chicago, Illinois

For information, address the publisher:
Raintree, 100 N. LaSalle, Suite 1200, Chicago, IL 60602

Printed and bound in the United States at Lake Book Manufacturing, Inc.
07 06
10 9 8 7 6 5 4 3 2

Library of Congress Cataloging-in-Publication Data:
Hughes, Monica.
  My Christmas / Monica Hughes.
     p. cm. -- (Festivals)
Summary: Illustrations and simple text describe how one family
celebrates Christmas.
Includes bibliographical references and index.
  ISBN 1-4109-0639-6 (library binding) -- ISBN 1-4109-0665-5 (pbk.)
  1. Christmas--Juvenile literature. [1. Christmas. 2. Holidays.] I.
Title. II. Series: Hughes, Monica. Festivals.
  GT4985.5.H84 2003
  394.2663--dc21
                          2003010844

Acknowledgments
The Publishers would like to thank p. 8 Chris Schwarz and Andes Press Agency; p. 16 Corbis for permission
to reproduce photographs.

Cover photograph of the children in costumes, reproduced with permission of Chris Schwarz

Every effort has been made to contact copyright holders of any material reproduced in this book.
Any omissions will be rectified in subsequent printings if notice is given to the publishers.

Some words are shown in bold, **like this.** You can find out
what they mean by looking in the glossary on page 24.

Contents

Christmas Is Coming!

Christmas is on December 25.

I count the days on the

advent calendar.

There is a treat in each window of the calendar.

Getting Ready

My sister and I make Christmas decorations.

My family saves money to help people.

Christmas Shopping

We go to the stores.

Look at all the Christmas lights!

We buy
presents for
our family.

9

A Visit to Santa

We go to visit Santa. We tell Santa what we want for Christmas.

My sister wants this big toy bear.

11

Our Christmas Tree

My father and I pick out the best tree.

Then, we put on the decorations.

Christmas Cards

Merry Christmas

We mail Christmas cards to our friends.

These are the cards our friends sent us.

At Church

This is a **nativity scene.**

It tells the Christmas story.

I dress like a **shepherd** for the nativity play.

My sister dresses like a sheep.

17

Christmas Day

We eat special treats on Christmas Day.

We play games with
our grandparents.

Christmas Dinner

We are having turkey for Christmas dinner.

There is lots of
other food, too.

Christmas Presents

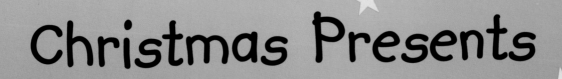

Time to open our Christmas presents!

This is our present for Mom and Dad.

Merry Christmas!

Glossary

advent calendar a special calendar with windows or doors for each day December 1 to December 25. Some advent calendars have candy or toys in each window or door.

nativity scene a small barn with people and animals that shows Jesus' birth in a stable on Christmas eve

shepherd person whose job is taking care of sheep

Index